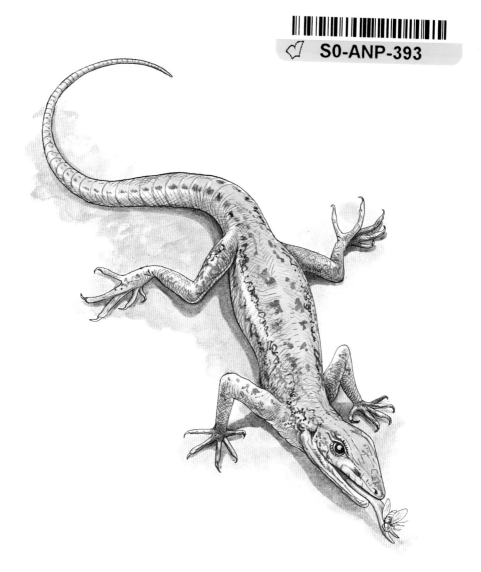

A lizard has a slim
body and a long tail.
Lizards feed on insects.

Lizards hatch from eggs,
which are laid in the soil
or hidden under rocks.

Lizards need the sun.  This is a common lizard sitting in the sun.

In the tropics, lizards live in the houses and catch bugs and insects.

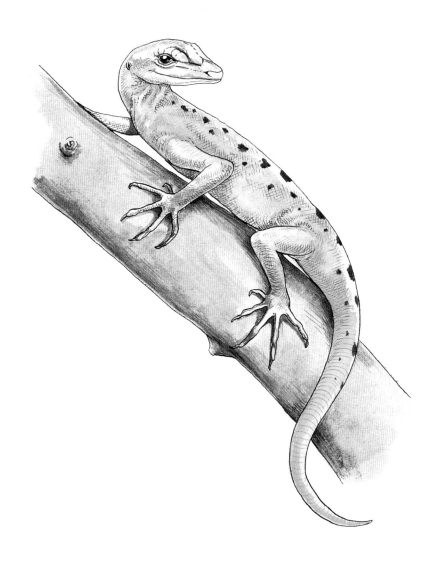

Shinning skinks can run up
steep rocks and tree trunks.

The ring-tailed dragon
runs on its back legs and
jumps, to catch insects.

The basilisk lizard runs on its back legs too. It can run across the top of a pond or river for several steps, without sinking.

The frilled lizard has a big flap of skin around its neck.

If it is attacked, it raises
its frill, to look bigger.

This lizard is a thorny devil.
It lives in deserts and feeds on ants.

If a lizard is attacked, it can shed its tail. The lizard runs free, and just its tail is left.

The lizard lives on and soon
its tail will develop again!